Contents

Health, Nutrition, and P.E. 1–2, SV 1419023578

Introduction

The school curriculum designates the topics taught to students. Health is one of the subjects that teachers should target. However, most stress is put on the core subjects, which leaves little time for this important area. An increased interest in the health of Americans has led to a revised interest in promoting health in the classroom.

Research suggests that the greatest threats to the health of Americans today are lifestyle diseases, such as cardiovascular disease and cancer. Among children, injuries claim more lives than disease. The facts that determine the length and quality of an individual's life are most often personal choices in several areas: diet, exercise, and personal cleanliness; the use of tobacco, alcohol, and other drugs; and the application of new health information to one's own habits. Responsibility for maintaining health and for minimizing the risk of developing chronic and degenerative diseases and disorders rests with the individual and begins early in life.

To achieve this goal, health education should promote positive attitudes, consistent positive behaviors, and good decision-making skills, which will contribute to good health and long-range prevention of disease. Effective health education should combine content and skill practice in a meaningful way that is applicable to daily life. Thus, health education is really life education. *Health, Nutrition, and P.E.* provides content and skills practice that will benefit all children. The activity pages address health concepts that can be applied on a personal level.

Organization

Health, Nutrition, and P.E. is divided into three units.

- **Unit 1** provides information on growth, the body, hygiene, drugs, and safety practices.
- **Unit 2** introduces information on nutrition. It includes background about the new food pyramid and healthy food selections.
- **Unit 3** explores fitness and exercise concepts. It offers activity pages explaining the benefits of exercise as well as specific, hands-on exercise suggestions.

Additional Notes

- **Correlation Chart**   A correlation chart can be found on pages 3 and 4. At a glance, it can help you plan your curriculum to ensure that key health and physical education standards are being met.

- **Assessment**   A two-page assessment is found on pages 5 and 6. You can use the test as a diagnostic tool by administering it before students begin the activities. After completing the activities, you may wish to test students again to gauge their progress.

- **Teacher Resource**   Each unit begins with an introduction. The introduction provides background information important to completing some of the skill pages as well as gives an overview of the concepts students will explore.

- **Bulletin Board**   A bulletin board idea accompanies each unit. The idea is either student-created or interactive, which meets standards required for classroom decoration. Detailed instructions explain how to build the board. Patterns are also provided.

Standards Correlation Chart

Standards	Pages
Health	
Explains actions an individual can take when not feeling well	41, 59, 60
Describes and demonstrates personal health habits	34, 35, 36, 37, 38, 39, 61, 62, 75, 76, 85, 86, 87, 88, 93, 94
Identifies and demonstrates the use of the five senses	23, 24
Identifies food groups and describes the effects of eating too much sugar and fat	67, 68, 69, 73, 75
Identifies healthy and unhealthy food choices	49, 67, 68, 69, 70, 71, 72, 73, 74, 75, 76, 77, 78
Defines stress and describes healthy behaviors that reduce stress	89
Demonstrates ways to communicate care, consideration, and respect of self and others	19, 20, 22, 89
Describes the importance of individual health maintenance activities	34, 35, 36, 37, 38, 39, 43, 44, 61, 62, 75, 76, 84, 85, 86, 87, 89
Identifies and describes the harmful effects of alcohol, tobacco, and other drugs on the body	45, 46, 47, 48, 49
Identifies ways to avoid deliberate and accidental injuries	25, 85, 86
Explains the need to use protective equipment when engaging in certain recreational activities	25, 62
Identifies the major body structures and organs of the body and describes their primary function	24, 25, 26, 27, 28, 29, 30, 31, 32, 33, 84, 85, 86, 87
Identifies the major systems of the body	28, 29, 30
Explains in which ways germs are transmitted, methods of preventing the spread of germs, and the importance of immunization	38, 39, 44, 62
Applies practices to control spread of germs in daily life	38, 39, 62
Identifies personal responsibilities as a family member in promoting and practicing healthy behaviors	21, 50, 75, 76, 85, 86, 87, 88
Identifies characteristics needed to be a responsible family member or friend	21, 22, 93, 94
Sets a personal health goal and tracks progress toward its achievement	35, 44, 75, 90

Standards Correlation Chart continued

Standards	Pages
Physical Education	
Demonstrates simple stunts that exhibit personal agility such as jumping one- and two-foot takeoffs and landing with good control	85, 86, 91, 92
Participates in appropriate exercises for flexibility in shoulders, legs, and trunk	85, 86, 91, 92
Identifies how regular physical activity strengthens the heart, lungs, and muscular system	84, 87, 93, 94
Identifies safe cycling and road practices	57
Describes appropriate reactions to emergency situations	50, 51, 52, 53, 54, 55, 56, 58

Name _____ Date _____

Assessment

 Darken the circle next to the best answer.

1. Faces can tell how people
_____
- Ⓐ think.
- Ⓑ feel.
- Ⓒ eat.
- Ⓓ exercise.

2. Your _____ tell you about
your world.
- Ⓐ heart
- Ⓑ head
- Ⓒ muscles
- Ⓓ senses

3. Your bones help you _____
- Ⓐ see.
- Ⓑ hear.
- Ⓒ move.
- Ⓓ breathe.

4. You get energy from _____
- Ⓐ exercise.
- Ⓑ food.
- Ⓒ smelling.
- Ⓓ sleeping.

5. What part of your teeth can
you see?
- Ⓐ root
- Ⓑ pulp
- Ⓒ dentin
- Ⓓ enamel

6. You can get rid of germs by
_____
- Ⓐ washing your hands.
- Ⓑ eating sweet food.
- Ⓒ running every day.
- Ⓓ wearing a bike helmet.

7. If your clothes catch on fire,
you should _____
- Ⓐ run to find an adult.
- Ⓑ get some water.
- Ⓒ stop, drop, and roll.
- Ⓓ yell loudly.

8. To stay safe on a bike, always
_____
- Ⓐ wear a helmet.
- Ⓑ ride in the road.
- Ⓒ ride as fast as you can.
- Ⓓ use turn lights.

Go on to the next page.

5

Assessment, p. 2

9. The _____ tells you how much of different foods to eat each day.
   - Ⓐ Sweet Circle
   - Ⓑ Fruit Square
   - Ⓒ Food Pyramid
   - Ⓓ Vegetable Rectangle

10. You should not eat too many _____
   - Ⓐ oils.
   - Ⓑ fruits.
   - Ⓒ vegetables.
   - Ⓓ meats.

11. _____ belong to the grains group.
   - Ⓐ Apples
   - Ⓑ Candies
   - Ⓒ Breads
   - Ⓓ Cheeses

12. Your heart and lungs become stronger when you _____
   - Ⓐ breathe.
   - Ⓑ brush your teeth.
   - Ⓒ wear clean clothes.
   - Ⓓ exercise.

Health for children revolves around a basic understanding of the functions of the human body and good health practices. By learning about their body, children can more easily understand why they should make healthy choices. It is never too early to begin healthy habits in hygiene, drugs, and safety. The habits children form will affect their life for many years to come.

Body Systems

There are twelve systems that work together to form the most amazing machine—the human body. During early elementary grades, children are introduced to four systems: digestive, circulatory, nervous, and respiratory. They learn the names and functions of the most important organs in these systems and why they are important to their health. However, all twelve systems are briefly described on this page and on page 8.

Skeletal System   The adult skeleton is a framework of 206 bones that fit together. It holds up the body and gives it shape. It also protects the internal organs and allows the body to move.

Muscular System   This system is made up of more than 600 muscles whose primary job is to move the body by contraction, or pulling. There are two main kinds of muscles: skeletal muscles and smooth muscles. Skeletal muscles, also known as voluntary muscles, are connected to the bones and can consciously be controlled. Smooth muscles, or involuntary muscles, contract automatically. The heart is a third kind of muscle, known as the cardiac muscle.

Digestive System   Digestion is the process by which food is broken down into particles, which provide energy and nutrients needed by the body to function. Digestion begins in the mouth, where teeth break the food. Saliva moistens it and begins the chemical breakdown. The food moves through the esophagus and then into the stomach, where it is broken down into a liquid. The food then moves into the small intestine, where acids and enzymes further process the food into substances for the body's use. Waste products are then moved through the large intestine.

Respiratory System   The respiratory system is responsible for breathing. Its main functions are to take in oxygen and remove carbon dioxide. Air enters the body through the nose and moves through the bronchial tubes into the lungs.

Circulatory System   This system moves blood throughout the body. Blood is essential since it carries food and oxygen for life, as well as removes carbon dioxide and wastes. The heart is the most important organ in this system.

Lymphatic System   This system works in conjunction with the circulatory system. Many white blood cells are found in the lymph nodes and are responsible for protecting the body from disease.

Reproductive System   The reproductive organs allow humans to have children. A sperm cell from a male joins with an egg cell from a female to produce a fertilized egg that develops into a human being.

Urinary System   In this system, liquid wastes are removed from the body. Blood moves through two kidneys that filter out water with other particles. The water travels through tubes to be excreted in the form of urine.

Health, Nutrition, and P.E. 1–2, SV 1419023578

Endocrine System   The endocrine system of glands produces a variety of hormones that regulate growth, reproduction, and food use.

Nervous System   This system is responsible for controlling and coordinating all the systems in the body. The brain is the nerve center that receives and understands messages. It reacts and tells the body what to do. The five senses fall under this system.

Integumentary System   The integumentary system is a smaller system made up of the skin, hair, nails, and sweat glands. The skin is actually an organ and is the largest one in the body.

Immune System   This system protects the body from disease. Organs, tissues, cells, and secretions from a variety of the body's systems play a role in immunity.

Staying Healthy

Staying healthy involves many factors, from making good, healthy choices in hygiene to visiting doctors on a regular basis for checkups and vaccine maintenance.

Hygiene   Hygiene involves keeping the body clean. For elementary students, stress should be placed on personal cleanliness, including dental and body care. Routine habits developed at a young age can prevent many health problems later in life.

Illness   Many times children get grumpy when they are ill. They may not be aware of how their body changes during illness. Encouraging them to listen to their body is an important step to help them understand illness. Once children focus on how their body changes when they are ill, they should be given a vocabulary to communicate their illness.

Drugs   For children, the word *drug* is often presented in the context of a harmful substance to be avoided. However, prescribed and over-the-counter medicines are drugs, too. A distinction should be made between healthful medicines, given by doctors and trusted adults, and harmful chemicals. In early elementary grades, discussion should be about harmful chemicals, which include tobacco and alcohol.

Safety

Elementary children can begin to understand many kinds of safety practices and the steps that should be followed for each. From the beginning, children should learn specific emergency information, including family members' names and their home addresses and phone numbers. Children should also learn how to talk on the phone with emergency personnel. Other important safety subjects that should be covered include fire, electrical, bike, and animal practices and rules.

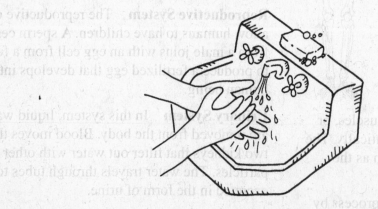

Health, Nutrition, and P.E. 1–2, SV 1419023578

Bulletin Board: Choose a Path to Good Health

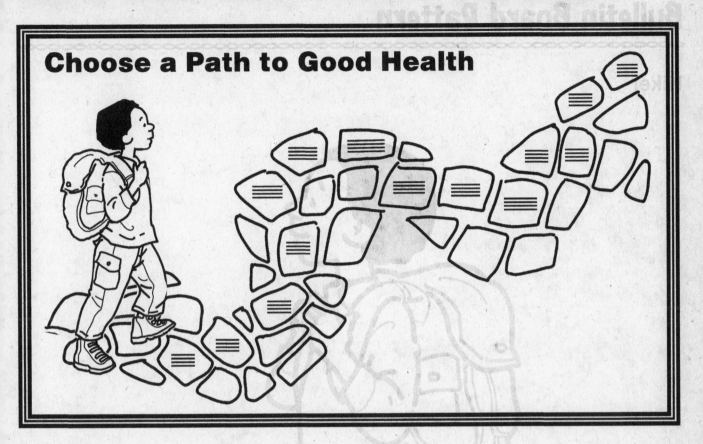

Choose a Path to Good Health

Materials

hiker pattern (page 10)
craft sticks
tape

white and tan construction paper
white and green craft paper
markers

scissors
stapler

Teacher Directions

1. Prepare a bulletin board with green paper. Add the title "Choose a Path to Good Health."
2. Enlarge and trace a hiker on white craft paper. Color and cut out the hiker.
3. Place the hiker near the bottom left corner of the board. Staple the figure to the board.
4. Trace many copies of a stone on tan paper.
5. Duplicate several hikers on white paper. Color and cut them out. Tape each hiker to a craft stick.
6. Cut out several stones and write sentences about bad health choices on them.
7. Mix together the stones students create with the ones completed in step 6. Use them to form a path on the board.
8. Invite students to move a hiker along the path to good health.

Student Directions

1. Cut out a tan stone.
2. Write a sentence that tells a way to stay healthy.

Health, Nutrition, and P.E. 1–2, SV 1419023578

Bulletin Board Pattern

Hiker

Health, Nutrition, and P.E. 1–2, SV 1419023578

Name _____ Date _____

Name _____ Date _____

How Have You Changed?

At first, babies just eat and sleep. They grow and change very quickly, though. Within a year, they are walking, talking, and eating all kinds of food. They are no longer babies!

 You Will Need

- baby picture
- mirror
- crayons

 Do This

A. Bring your baby picture to school.

B. Look in the mirror.

C. Draw a picture of yourself now below.

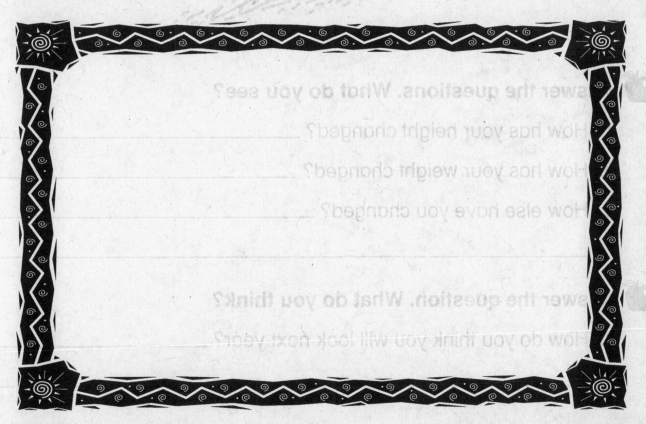

Go on to the next page.

Unit 1: Health
Health, Nutrition, and P.E. 1–2, SV 1419023578

How Have You Changed?, p. 2

Answer the questions. What do you see?

1. How has your height changed? _____

2. How has your weight changed? _____

3. How else have you changed? _____

   _____

Answer the question. What do you think?

4. How do you think you will look next year? _____

   _____

   _____

Health, Nutrition, and P.E. 1–2, SV 1419023578

Growing Up

 Look at the pictures. Order the pictures from youngest to oldest. Write numbers under the pictures to show the correct order.

A. _____   B. _____   C. _____

D. _____   E. _____   F. _____

Unit 1: Health
Health, Nutrition, and P.E. 1–2, SV 1419023578

When I Was a Baby

When you were a baby, you were almost helpless. Someone had to take care of you all the time. Humans take a long time to grow into adults that can care for themselves. Yet even as a baby you could do a few things for yourself.

 Answer the questions.

1. What things could you do for yourself when you were a baby?

   _____

   _____

2. What things did your parents have to do for you?

   _____

   _____

3. What are some of the things you have learned to do by yourself?

   _____

   _____

4. Even though you can do many things for yourself, you still need your parents. What are the things your parents do to help you?

   _____

   _____

5. What are some things you cannot do now, but you hope to do when you are older?

   _____

   _____

Health, Nutrition, and P.E. 1–2, SV 1419023578

Name _____ Date _____ Date _____

When I Grow Up!

 Complete the sentences. Then, draw a picture of yourself as a grown-up.

When I grow up, I will be able to _____

and _____.

I will have _____

and _____.

I will not have to _____

or _____.

Health, Nutrition, and P.E. 1–2, SV 1419023578

Ways We Grow

 Read the chart. Read the words below the chart. Write the letter of the words under the correct heading on the chart.

Bodies Growing	Learning Things	Being Responsible

A. shoes too small

B. can tie shoes

C. clothes too small

D. can read

E. putting away toys

F. can write

G. setting the table

H. baby teeth fall out

I. keeping room neat

Health, Nutrition, and P.E. 1–2, SV 1419023578

Name _____ Date _____

How Do You Measure Up?

Look at your friends. They all have different heights. One person may grow faster in the beginning. This person may end up shorter than someone else who started growing later.

🍎 **Work with 4 classmates. Measure each other. Fill in the chart.**

Height Chart

Classmate	Height (in inches)
Me	
Friend 1	
Friend 2	
Friend 3	
Friend 4	

Go on to the next page.

How Do You Measure Up?, p. 2

 Use the information in the chart to make a bar graph.

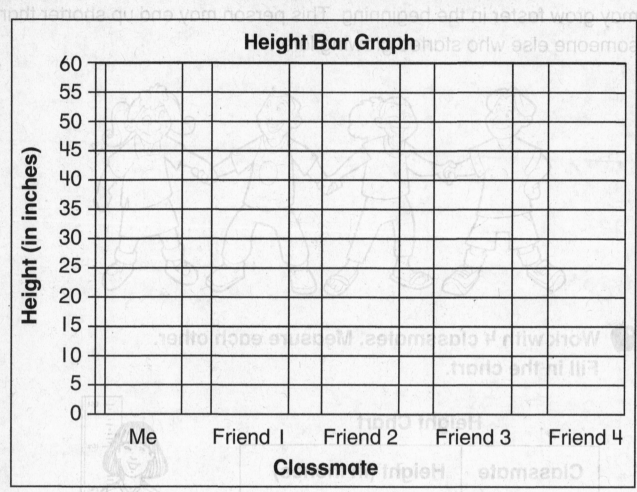

Height Bar Graph

 Answer the questions.

1. Who was the tallest person? _____

2. Who was the shortest person? _____

3. What was the difference in height between the tallest and

   shortest person? _____

4. Write the names of the people in order from shortest to tallest.

   _____

Health, Nutrition, and P.E. 1–2, SV 1419023578

Name _____ Date _____

Feelings

People can have many different feelings. They can be happy or sad. They can be afraid or proud. Faces can tell you how people feel.

🍎 **Read each story. Look at the faces. Draw a line from each story to the face that matches it.**

1. Jason's little brother dropped Jason's crayon box. The crayons are broken.

A.

2. Jason's mother said that she would help Jason make a kite in a little while. "It's time now!" Jason's mother says.

B.

3. Jason is about to fall asleep at night. He hears a strange noise.

C.

4. Jason's best friend moved to another town. Jason has no one to play with.

D.

Health, Nutrition, and P.E. 1–2, SV 1419023578

I Have Feelings

 Complete each sentence.

1. I am happy when

_____

_____

2. I am proud when

_____

_____

3. I am sad when

_____

_____

4. I am afraid when

_____

_____

5. I am angry when

_____

_____

Health, Nutrition, and P.E. 1–2, SV 1419023578

Name _____ Date _____

Family Feelings

 Circle the letter of the sentence that tells about each picture.

1. **A.** Family members like to talk and laugh when they are together.

   B. Family members get angry at each other when they are together.

2. **A.** Family members make fun of each other.

   B. Family members help each other when someone is sad.

3. **A.** Family members show love.

   B. Family members hurt one another's feelings.

Unit 1: Health
Health, Nutrition, and P.E. 1–2, SV 1419023578

Name _____ Date _____

Solving Conflicts

When people do not agree, they have a conflict, or problem. It is important to solve conflicts. There are four steps that can help you solve conflicts.

 The steps to resolving a conflict below are out of order. On the lines, write the steps in the correct order.

> Agree to disagree.
> Find a way for both sides to win.
> Talk about a solution.
> Stop.

Step 1

_____

_____

Step 2

_____

_____

Step 3

_____

_____

Step 4

_____

_____

Health, Nutrition, and P.E. 1–2, SV 1419023578

The Five Senses

How do you learn about things? You use your senses. Your senses tell you about your world. The senses are seeing, hearing, smelling, tasting, and touching.

 Decide which sense you use to identify each thing. Draw a line to match the thing in the left column with the correct sense in the right column.

1.

2.

3.

4.

5.

Health, Nutrition, and P.E. 1–2, SV 1419023578

Name _____ Date _____

Date _____

Your Eyes

 Follow the directions.

1. Draw a line to match each name with the correct eye part.
Then color the eyes to match your eye color.

A. pupil **B.** iris

 Answer the questions.

2. What do your eyes look like when it is dark?

3. What do your eyes look like when there is bright light?

4. How do your eyes help you?

_____

_____

Health, Nutrition, and P.E. 1–2, SV 1419023578

Matching Bones

There are bones under your skin. Your bones fit together to make your skeleton. Your skeleton holds up your body and gives it shape. Some skeleton bones help you move. Other bones keep the parts inside your body safe.

 Match the bones to the places where they are found. Draw lines from the pictures of bones to the parts of the girl's body.

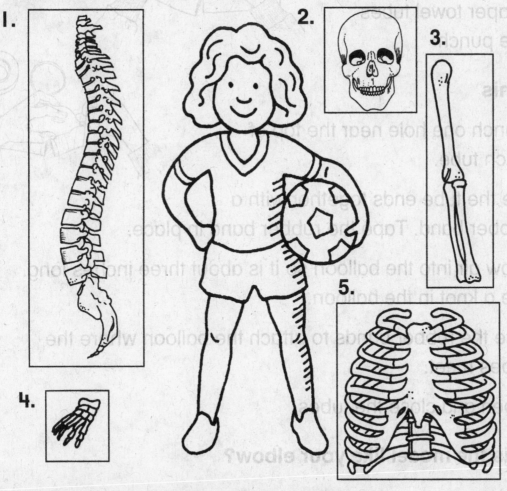

 The girl is going to play soccer. Draw something on her that will help keep her leg bones from getting hurt.

Make a Model Elbow

Muscles are body parts that work to move your bones. One muscle pulls a bone to move it. Then the other muscle pulls the bone to move it back.

 You Will Need

- tube balloon
- masking tape
- 3 rubber bands
- 2 paper towel tubes
- hole punch

 Do This

1. Punch one hole near the top of each tube.

2. Tie the tube ends together with a rubber band. Tape the rubber band in place.

3. Blow air into the balloon so it is about three inches long. Tie a knot in the balloon.

4. Use the rubber bands to attach the balloon where the tubes meet.

5. Open and close the tubes.

 How is the model like your elbow?

_____

_____

Health, Nutrition, and P.E. 1–2, SV 1419023578

Name _____ Date _____

Muscles and Nerves

Muscles are body parts that move your bones. Nerves are body parts that help you learn about your world. They send messages to the brain.

 Answer each question by writing muscles or nerves.

1. We need to stretch gently before exercise.

   What are we?

   _____

2. We tell you about your world.

   What are we?

   _____

3. We make your muscles work.

   What are we?

   _____

4. You use us to blink, run, and eat.

   What are we?

   _____

5. We are joined to the brain.

   What are we?

   _____

Name _____   Date _____

Digesting Food

Your body needs food to give you energy. To get energy, your body must digest, or break down, the food.

 Draw lines to match each body part to what it does.

What It Is

1. mouth

2. stomach

3. tongue

4. teeth

What It Does

A. chew the food

B. takes food into the body

C. crushes food and turns it into a thick liquid

D. tastes food and pushes it into the throat

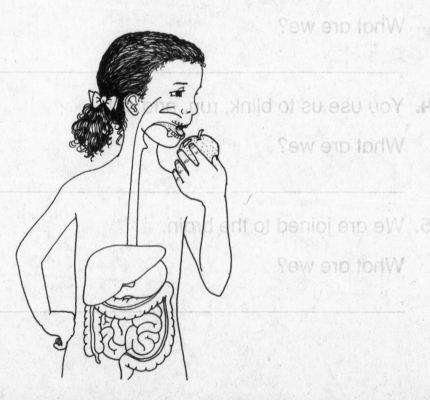

Health, Nutrition, and P.E. 1–2, SV 1419023578

Name _____ Date _____

Investigate Digestion

When you digest food, your body breaks it down. You begin to digest food in your mouth. When you chew your food, it mixes with saliva. Saliva is the liquid in your mouth that begins to break down food.

 You Will Need

- 1 cracker
- mirror
- paper
- pencil

 Do This

1. Look at the cracker. Draw a picture of it.

2. Put the cracker in your mouth. Do not chew it. Count slowly to 20.

3. Think about how the cracker feels. Use the mirror to look at it.

4. Draw what the cracker looks like.

 What happened to the cracker?

_____

_____

_____

Health, Nutrition, and P.E. 1–2, SV 1419023578

Name _____ Date _____

Your Heart

Your heart is a muscle. It is about the size of your fist. Each time your heart beats, it pumps blood through tubes called vessels. The blood vessels go to all parts of your body. The blood carries oxygen. Then the blood returns to the heart to get more oxygen.

🍎 **Color the heart and blood vessels red.**

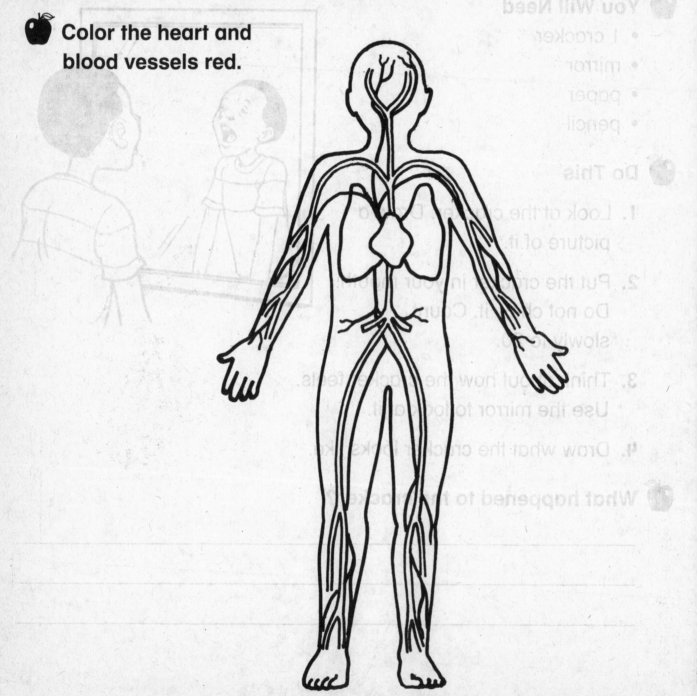

Unit 1: Health
Health, Nutrition, and P.E. 1–2, SV 1419023578

Name _____ Date _____

Investigate Your Heart

Your heart rate is how fast or slowly your heart beats. When you exercise, your heart beats faster. Your heart rate is faster. When you rest, your heart rate is slower.

 You Will Need

- paper cup
- scissors
- clock with second hand

 Do This

1. Work with a partner. Cut the bottom out of a paper cup.

2. Take turns. Use the paper cup to listen to each other's heart for one minute. Count the beats. Record the number in the chart below.

3. Choose one partner to go first. Jump up and down for one minute. Have the other person listen to the heart to count the beats. Record the number in the chart below.

4. Repeat step 3 with the other partner.

Name	Resting Heartbeat	Active Heartbeat

 How did the heartbeat change?

_____

_____

Health, Nutrition, and P.E. 1–2, SV 1419023578

Name _____ Date _____

Name _____ Date _____

Parts of a Tooth

Your teeth help you eat. Some teeth cut food. Some teeth crush food. Other teeth rip food. But all teeth are made the same.

 Look at the diagram of the tooth. Color each part of the diagram. Use the right color for each part.

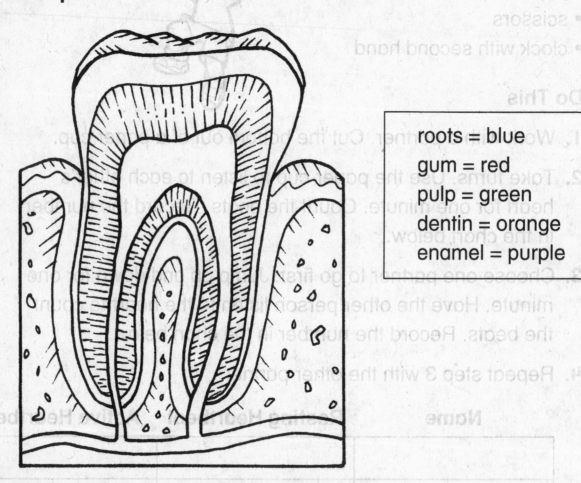

roots = blue
gum = red
pulp = green
dentin = orange
enamel = purple

 What part of the tooth can you see in your mouth? Write the name.

_____

Health, Nutrition, and P.E. 1–2, SV 1419023578

Tooth Facts

When you were born, you had no teeth showing above the gum. By the time you started kindergarten, you had all 20 primary teeth. You have probably started to lose some of these baby teeth already. Now you have some permanent teeth growing in. By the time you are a young adult, you may have all 32 permanent teeth.

🍎 **Read the facts. Write numbers beside the facts to show the order in which people grow teeth.**

_____ **A.** You have no teeth showing above the gum.

_____ **B.** You have some permanent teeth growing in.

_____ **C.** You have 20 primary teeth.

🍎 **Complete the sentences.**

1. Babies don't have teeth, so they can't _____.

2. I have teeth, so I can _____.

Tooth Care

Taking care of your teeth is very important. You want your teeth to be healthy and strong. You do not want cavities. Cavities are holes in the teeth. Here are some rules for keeping your teeth healthy.

- Brush your teeth every morning and before bed.
- Use a toothbrush that is soft.
- Visit the dentist twice a year.
- Eat lots of fruits and dairy foods.
- Do not eat a lot of sweets.

 Circle the pictures that show healthy tooth habits.

Name _____ Date _____

Healthy Teeth

 Do you follow all these habits? Keep this chart for one week. At the end of each day, put a check mark by the habits you followed that day.

	Mon.	Tues.	Wed.	Thurs.	Fri.	Sat.	Sun.
Brushed my teeth in the morning							
Brushed my teeth in the evening							
Ate dairy products							
Ate fruit							
Brushed or rinsed mouth after eating							
Did not eat a lot of sweets							

Health, Nutrition, and P.E. 1–2, SV 1419023578

Name _____ Date _____

Dental Hygiene

≈≈

Dental hygiene means keeping your mouth healthy. You must be sure to brush and floss your teeth. You should also see a dentist for checkups. These things will keep your teeth and gums healthy.

 Do you have healthy tooth habits? Fill in the chart below.

Habit	Yes	No
Do you eat healthy meals?		
Do you eat healthy snacks?		
Do you brush your teeth after every meal?		
Do you brush your teeth at least twice a day?		
Do you floss your teeth every day?		
Do you visit the dentist?		

 Look at the chart. What can you do to be more healthy?

_____

_____

_____

≈≈

Health, Nutrition, and P.E. 1–2, SV 1419023578

Name _____ Date _____

Staying Healthy

 Look at the pictures. Use words from the box to complete each sentence.

| teeth | food | bed | wash |

1.  Use soap to _____ every day.

2.  Brush your _____.

3.  Eat healthy _____.

4.  Go to _____ early.

Health, Nutrition, and P.E. 1–2, SV 1419023578

Name _____   Date _____

Hygiene Health

～～～～～～～～～～～～～～～～～～～～～～～

Hygiene is what you do to keep your body clean. A clean body means that you will be more healthy. There will be fewer germs to make you sick.

 Look at each picture. Tell how it shows good hygiene. Use complete sentences. Then answer the question.

1.

_____
_____
_____
_____

2.

_____
_____
_____
_____

3.

_____
_____
_____
_____

4. What is another good hygiene rule?

_____
_____

～～～～～～～～～～～～～～～～～～～～～～～

Unit 1: Health
Health, Nutrition, and P.E. 1–2, SV 1419023578

Stop Those Germs

Germs are small things that you cannot see. They can grow in and on your body. Germs can make you sick. There are things you should do to keep germs off your body.

🍎 **Read each sentence. Circle the T if the sentence is true. Circle the F if the sentence is false.**

T   F   1. Using soap helps fight germs.

T   F   2. You should wash your hands after you touch an animal.

T   F   3. You should wash your hands after you sneeze.

T   F   4. Germs are easy to see.

T   F   5. Fingernails do not need to be cleaned or trimmed.

🍎 **Choose one false sentence. Rewrite it to make it true.**

6. _____

_____

_____

    Health, Nutrition, and P.E. 1–2, SV 1419023578

Name _____ Date _____ Date _____

Who Is Ill?

Sometimes you may not feel well. Your nose is red. You cannot breathe. You might even feel very cold. You could be ill.

 Circle the pictures that show children who are ill.

Unit 1: Health
Health, Nutrition, and P.E. 1–2, SV 1419023578

Name _____ Date _____

Communicate When You Are Ill

You need to know what to say when you tell someone you are ill. Before talking to an adult, think about how your body feels. Where do you hurt? What is different about your body?

 Read the feelings in the first column. Read sentences to say in the second column. Draw a line to match each feeling with a sentence you should say.

How You Feel

1. hot and weak

2. pain or pressure in your head

3. like throwing up

4. like the room is spinning

5. hurts when you swallow

What You Say

A. "I am sick to my stomach."

B. "I have a fever."

C. "I have a sore throat."

D. "I am dizzy."

E. "I have a headache."

Health, Nutrition, and P.E. 1–2, SV 1419023578

Illness Words

 Read the words in the box. Use them to complete the puzzle.

| ill   asthma   disease   allergy   head lice   vaccines |

Across

1. An illness caused by a reaction in the body

3. Tiny bugs that lay eggs in the hair

4. Shots or pills to keep people from getting some diseases

Down

1. An illness that makes it hard to breathe

2. Another name for illness

5. Not well

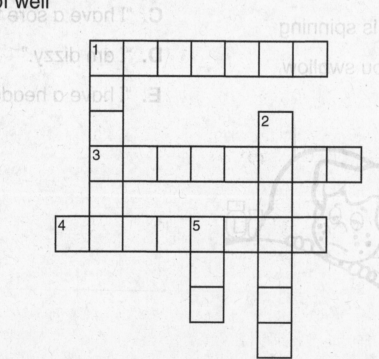

Health, Nutrition, and P.E. 1–2, SV 1419023578

Name _____ Date _____

Date _____

A Healthy Checkup

 Draw lines to match each sentence with the correct picture.

1. The doctor checks your ears.

A.

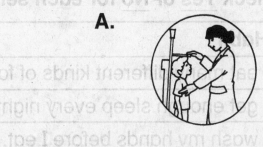

2. The doctor measures your height and weight.

B.

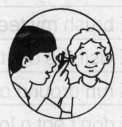

3. The doctor looks at your throat.

C.

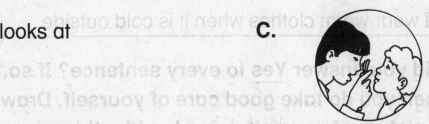

4. The doctor checks your eyes.

D.

5. The doctor listens to your heart.

E.

Health, Nutrition, and P.E. 1–2, SV 1419023578

Name _____   Date _____

Do You Take Good Care of Yourself?

Do you take good care of yourself? Take this test.

 Check <u>Yes</u> or <u>No</u> for each sentence.

Habit	Yes	No
I eat many different kinds of foods.		
I get enough sleep every night.		
I wash my hands before I eat.		
I brush my teeth every morning and night.		
I visit the dentist at least once a year.		
I run around and play each day.		
I don't eat a lot of candy and other sweets.		
I wear warm clothes when it is cold outside.		

 Did you answer <u>Yes</u> to every sentence? If so, then you do take good care of yourself. Draw a picture of yourself doing healthy things.

Health, Nutrition, and P.E. 1–2, SV 1419023578

Medicine Smart

When you are ill, you might have to take medicine. Medicine can make you feel better. But you must be careful with medicine.

 Read each story. Circle the letter that answers the question.

> **1.** Aunt Luisa put the medicine away. She put it in the top cabinet. No children can reach the medicine.

What is the story about?

A. Aunt Luisa can reach high places.

B. Aunt Luisa put the medicine in a safe place.

> **2.** Mother is helping Kaleel take medicine. "Hurry up," Kaleel says. "Just give me one spoonful."
>
> Mother says, "Wait, Kaleel. I need to read the instructions."

Why does Kaleel's mother want to wait?

A. She wants to give Kaleel the right amount of medicine.

B. She doesn't want Kaleel to feel better.

Health, Nutrition, and P.E. 1–2, SV 1419023578

Medicines and Drugs

~~~~~~

 Read the sentences. Write words from the box to complete them.

| medicines | caffeine | drugs | instructions |

I. Some soft drinks have a drug called _____.

2. When you must take medicine, it is important that an adult

read the _____ on the label.

3. Not all drugs are _____, but all _____

are drugs. (Hint: Use the same word two times.)

4. Caffeine and other _____ affect children more than

adults, because children have smaller bodies.

Unit 1: Health
Health, Nutrition, and P.E. 1–2, SV 1419023578

Name _____ Date _____

Don't Chew Tobacco!

Cigarettes are made from tobacco. Some tobacco is made to chew. Chewing tobacco contains nicotine, like other kinds of tobacco. Even though it is not smoked, chewing tobacco hurts the body.

 Follow the directions to show how chewing tobacco hurts the body.

1. Juice from chewing tobacco hurts the gums. Color the gums red.

2. Chewing tobacco can make the teeth loose. Color the teeth blue.

3. Chewing tobacco can cause cancer of the lips and tongue. Color the lips and tongue purple.

4. All tobacco causes bad breath. Use green to show bad breath.

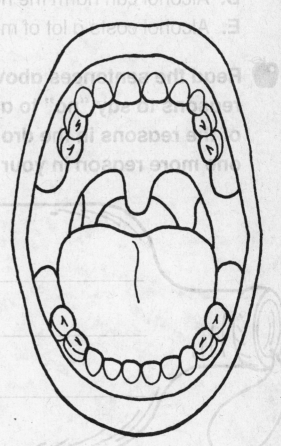

Health, Nutrition, and P.E. 1–2, SV 1419023578

Say No to Alcohol

Alcohol is a kind of drug. You should say "no" if someone asks you to drink alcohol. Here are some reasons you should not drink alcohol.

    A. Alcohol is a drug.

    B. Alcohol tastes bad.

    C. Alcohol is illegal for children.

    D. Alcohol can harm the heart.

    E. Alcohol costs a lot of money.

 Read the sentences above. Choose three reasons to say "no" to alcohol. Write the letters of the reasons in the drops. On the bottle, write one more reason in your own words.

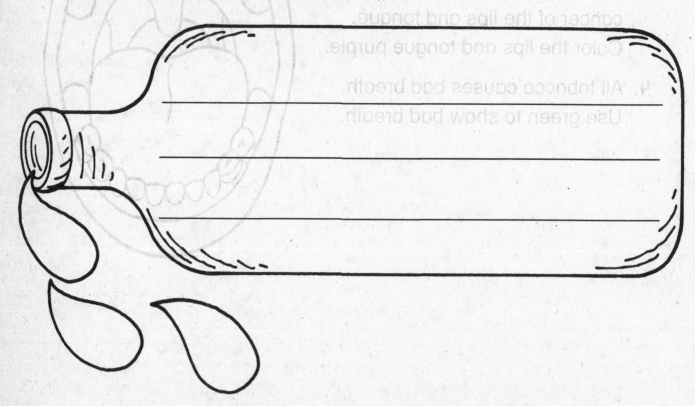

Health, Nutrition, and P.E. 1–2, SV 1419023578

Name _____ Date _____

Reading Food Labels

Caffeine is a kind of drug. It is found in coffee, tea, and sodas. A person who drinks caffeine can feel excited. Too much caffeine is not good for your body.

 Look at the labels on food products in your home. Find ones that have caffeine. Write the names of the foods in the chart. Then write the names of other foods that you could eat that are healthier choices.

Foods with Caffeine	Healthier Choices

Health, Nutrition, and P.E. 1–2, SV 1419023578

Name _____ Date _____

Know Those Numbers

∞∞∞∞∞∞∞∞∞∞∞∞∞∞∞∞∞∞∞∞∞∞∞∞∞∞∞∞∞∞∞∞∞∞

 Complete the form. Ask an adult to help.

Parent's name: _____

Address: _____

_____

Phone number: _____

Work number: _____

Neighbor's name: _____

Address: _____

Phone number: _____

Emergency Numbers

Police: _____

Fire: _____

Poison Control: _____

Doctor: _____

∞∞∞∞∞∞∞∞∞∞∞∞∞∞∞∞∞∞∞∞∞∞∞∞∞∞∞∞∞∞∞∞∞∞

Health, Nutrition, and P.E. 1–2, SV 1419023578

Fire Safety

Fires are dangerous. It is important to learn how to keep your home safe from fire.

🍎 **Read the fire safety rules.**

1. Wall outlets should not be overloaded. They can cause fires.

2. Cords should not be run under furniture. In these places, cords can easily be damaged. Damaged cords can start fires.

3. Space should be left around appliances. Then, heat can move away.

4. Things that burn easily, such as newspapers, should be kept away from any heat.

5. Fireplaces should be covered. Then sparks cannot fly out.

6. Every home should have a smoke detector. The detector can give a warning.

7. Have practice fire drills with your family. Make sure that stairs, hallways, and doors are not blocked.

8. The fire department phone number should be posted near every telephone in the house.

Go on to the next page.

Health, Nutrition, and P.E. 1–2, SV 1419023578

Fire Safety, p. 2

🍎 **Look at the picture below. Circle at least 7 things that do not follow the fire safety rules.**

FIRE DEPT.
555-1234

Health, Nutrition, and P.E. 1–2, SV 1419023578

Name _____ Date _____

Emergency! Emergency!

Suppose there is an emergency at your house. Would you know what to tell the 911 operator?

 Answer the questions.

911 Operator: What is the problem?

You: There is a fire at my house.

911 Operator: What is the address?

You: _____

911 Operator: What is your name?

You: _____

911 Operator: Is there anyone in the house?

You: _____

911 Operator: Is anyone hurt?

You: _____

911 Operator: Where are you?

You: _____

911 Operator: Stay in a safe place. Help is on the way!

Health, Nutrition, and P.E. 1–2, SV 1419023578

Name _____ Date _____

Stop, Drop, and Roll!

∞∞

If your clothes catch on fire, remember these three steps: **stop**, **drop**, and **roll**!

 Write stop, drop, and roll to show what is happening in each picture. Color the pictures and cut them out. Put the pictures in the correct order. Glue them on paper.

∞∞

Health, Nutrition, and P.E. 1–2, SV 1419023578

Electric Safety

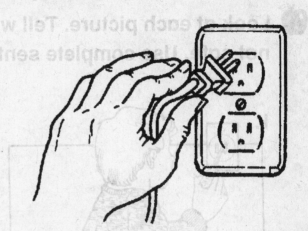

Electricity gives us light and heat. Electricity can be very dangerous. The electricity in a cord can kill. Here are some rules to keep you safe with electricity.

1. Keep fingers and other things out of the electric outlets.

2. Hold the plastic part of the plug when plugging in an appliance. Don't ever touch the metal part of the plug when it is near an outlet.

3. Cover outlets with plastic caps when not in use.

4. Check cords for cracks or breaks.

5. Keep electric appliances away from water.

6. Don't touch an appliance if you or your hands are wet.

 Answer the question.

Why do you think people cover outlets with caps?

_____

_____

_____

Health, Nutrition, and P.E. 1–2, SV 1419023578

Danger with Electricity

 Look at each picture. Tell why the person is not safe. Use complete sentences.

1.

_____

_____

_____

2.

_____

_____

_____

Health, Nutrition, and P.E. 1–2, SV 1419023578

Name _____ Date _____

Bicycle Safety Rules

1. Ride on the right-hand side of the street.

2. Obey all traffic signs.

3. Use hand signals.

4. Have a light on your bicycle if

   you ride at night.

   Wear light-colored clothing.

5. Always wear a helmet.

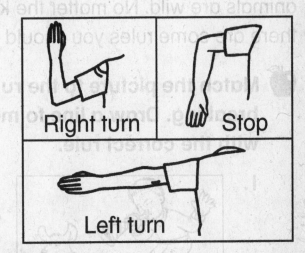

Right turn   Stop

Left turn

 Are these children following bicycle safety rules? Circle those who are. Put an X on those who are not.

Unit 1: Health
Health, Nutrition, and P.E. 1–2, SV 1419023578

Name _____ Date _____

Animal Safety

Many animals are fun to play with. Some animals are pets. Some animals are wild. No matter the kind of animal, if you do not know it, there are some rules you should follow.

 Match the picture to the rules the children are breaking. Draw a line to match each picture with the correct rule.

1.

2.

3.

4.

Rules

A. Never bother an animal when it is eating.

B. Never touch a wild animal.

C. Don't make loud noises around an animal.

D. Never tease an animal.

Unit 1: Health
Health, Nutrition, and P.E. 1–2, SV 1419023578

Name _____ Date _____

Name _____ Date _____

A Trip to the Hospital

Hospital Words

You or someone you know may have to go to the hospital. Doctors and nurses work in a hospital. They will help people who are sick or who need special care.

 Suppose a boy named Miguel does not feel good. He goes to the hospital. Read the sentences below. They tell what happens to Miguel when he goes to the hospital. Write the letters to put the sentences in the correct order.

1. First, _____

2. Next, _____

3. Then, _____

4. Then, _____

5. Finally, _____

Things That Happened

A. doctors and nurses work with Miguel's family to help him.

B. the nurse checks Miguel and asks questions about how he feels.

C. Miguel rides out of the hospital in a wheelchair.

D. Miguel gets a name bracelet.

E. Miguel may have tests to find out what is wrong.

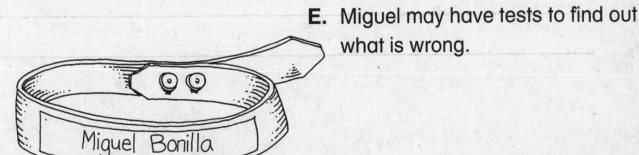

Miguel Bonilla

Hospital Words

 Color the puzzle pieces that contain an apple to find special hospital words. Then write what the word means on the lines below the puzzle.

1.

_____

_____

2.

_____

_____

Health, Nutrition, and P.E. 1–2, SV 1419023578

Name _____

Date _____

Yan's Healthy Choices

Yan likes to play basketball with his friends. He doesn't like to be ill. He makes healthy choices to stay well. Getting exercise is one good choice.

1

-------------------------------- Fold --------------------------------

Activity

What can you do to stay healthy? Draw a picture.

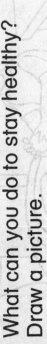

4

Health, Nutrition, and P.E. 1–2, SV 1419023578

Sometimes Yan goes to the doctor. He gets vaccines that keep him from getting diseases. Yan does not like the shots, but he knows the vaccines will help keep him healthy.

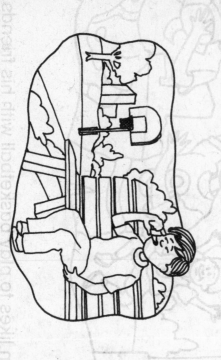

Yan washes his hands with soap. He gets rid of germs. He knows that germs can spread disease.

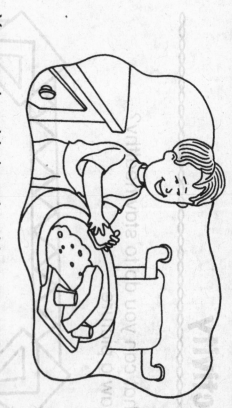

Yan has asthma. Sometimes it is hard for him to breathe. He takes medicine to help him stay healthy and keep playing.

Yan likes to ride bikes. He wears a helmet to stay safe. He follows all the bike rules, too.

2

3

Unit 1: Health
Health, Nutrition, and P.E. 1–2, SV 1419023578

Teacher Resource

Obesity is becoming a major concern of both children and adults. The large serving sizes of fast foods combined with a sedentary lifestyle are the prime reasons for increased weight. It is important for children to recognize that they can make choices that will help them live healthy lives. They need to learn the connections between what they eat and the way they look and feel. They need to have the basic information that will help them make good food choices.

The revised food pyramid offers a suggestion for maintaining a healthy lifestyle. It recommends serving sizes for each food group and oils based on individual needs. Eating the right amount of foods from each group every day provides a balanced diet. Eating too many foods from one group or not enough of another can lead to deficiencies or weight problems. Although vitamin supplements can help with these deficiencies, vitamins are best absorbed in the body naturally through the digestion of the foods that contain them.

Nutrition

The body needs to receive certain nutrients in order to grow and to stay healthy. These nutrients are broken down into six types: carbohydrates, proteins, fat, vitamins, minerals, and water.

Carbohydrates are sugars and starches. Sugar, such as fruits and honey, give the body quick energy, while the starches, such as bread, cereal, and rice, give the body stored energy.

Proteins come from foods such as milk, cheese, lean meat, fish, peas, and beans; they help the body to repair itself. Proteins are used by the body to build muscle and bone, and they give the body energy.

Fat is important for energy, too, and it helps to keep the body warm. If the body does not use the fats put into it, it will store the fat. Fats come from foods such as meat, milk, butter, oil, and nuts.

Vitamins are important to the body in many ways. Vitamins help the other nutrients in a person's body work together. Lack of certain vitamins can cause serious illnesses. Vitamin A, for example, which can be obtained from foods such as broccoli, carrots, and liver, helps with eyesight. Vitamin B, from green leafy vegetables, eggs, and milk, helps with growth and energy.

Minerals can be found in foods such as milk, vegetables, seafood, and raisins. They help the body grow. Calcium is a mineral that helps make strong bones, and iron is needed for healthy red blood.

Water makes up most of the human body and helps to keep the body's temperature normal. People should drink several glasses of water each day.

The Food Pyramid

A new food pyramid has recently been approved. Since each person is different in terms of age, sex, and exercise levels, the new food pyramid suggests daily dietary needs based on these characteristics. The web site www.mypyramid.gov not only gives serving suggestions and caloric intake, but the site offers a wealth of information, including a reminder to exercise daily. The five food groups plus oils guidelines have changed slightly. Point out that the width of the food group stripes on the pyramid suggests how much food a person should choose from each group. Encourage children to choose more foods from the food groups with the widest stripes. Encourage children to read food labels.

Grains are made from plants, such as wheat, corn, rice, oats, and barley. Servings of grains are given in ounces.

Vegetables include the plants as well as 100 percent juice. They can be served in any manner, raw or cooked. There are five vegetable subgroups: dark green, orange, dry beans and peas, starch, and other vegetables. The serving size for vegetables is given in cups.

Fruits, like vegetables, can be fresh, canned, or 100 percent juice. Eating a wide variety of colorful fruits is highly recommended. Serving sizes are also in cups.

Oils are to be used sparingly. We all need some oil. Oils are found in butter, margarine, nuts, fish,

and liquid oils such as corn, soybean, canola, and olive oil. Serving sizes are given in teaspoons.

Milk includes such foods as milk, cheese, yogurt, and ice cream. Skim and low-fat products are recommended to reduce the oil intake. Servings are given in cups.

Meat and Beans include fish, poultry, beef, eggs, nuts, and dried beans, such as navy beans and kidney beans. Serving sizes are given in ounces.

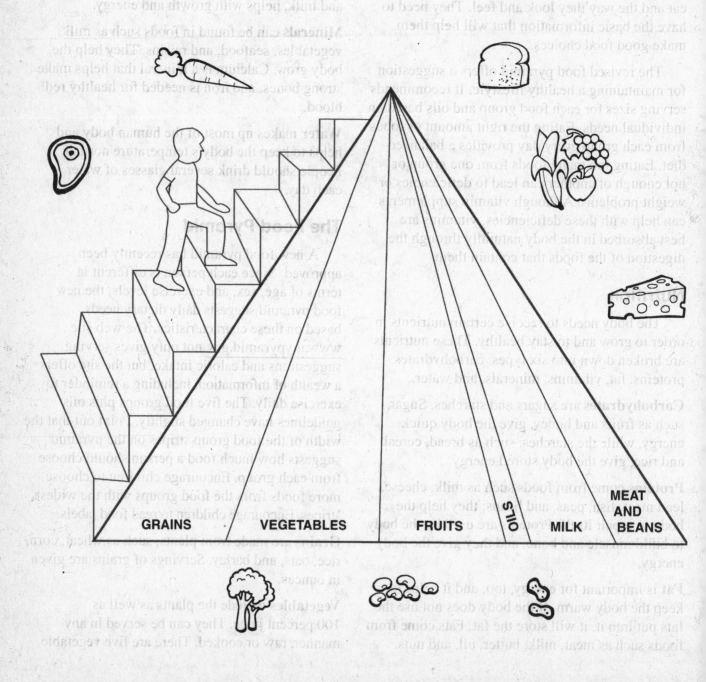

GRAINS   VEGETABLES   FRUITS   OILS   MILK   MEAT AND BEANS

Health, Nutrition, and P.E. 1–2, SV 1419023578

Bulletin Board: We Eat the Pyramid Way

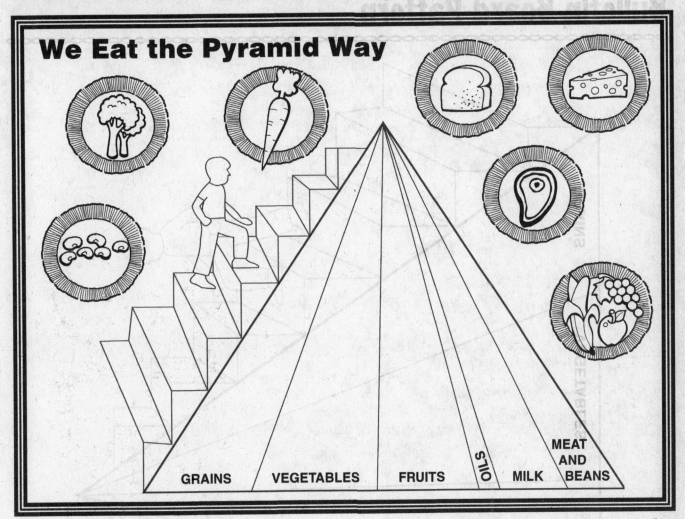

We Eat the Pyramid Way

GRAINS VEGETABLES FRUITS OILS MILK MEAT AND BEANS

Materials

food pyramid pattern (page 66)   recycled magazines   markers
craft paper   glue   scissors
large paper plates   stapler

Teacher Directions

1. Prepare a bulletin board with the desired color of craft paper. Add the title "We Eat the Pyramid Way."
2. Enlarge and trace the food pyramid on white craft paper. Color and cut out the pyramid.
3. Staple the pyramid in the center of the board.
4. Staple the completed paper plate meals to the board in a pleasing arrangement.

Student Directions

1. Cut out magazine pictures that show healthy foods. Choose a food that comes from each food group and oils on the pyramid.
2. Glue the foods to a plate.
3. Tell a friend about the foods on the plate. Name the section on the pyramid that each food would go in.

     Health, Nutrition, and P.E. 1–2, SV 1419023578

Bulletin Board Pattern

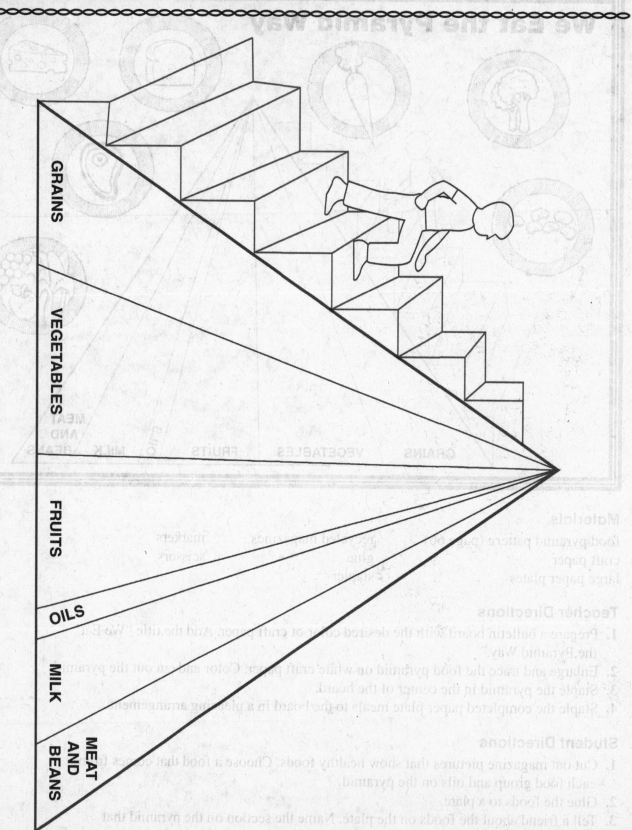

GRAINS

VEGETABLES

FRUITS

OILS

MILK

MEAT AND BEANS

Health, Nutrition, and P.E. 1–2, SV 1419023578

The Food Pyramid

The food pyramid shows five food groups and oils. The five food groups are very important. The groups are grains, vegetables, fruits, milk, and meat and beans. The foods in these groups help your body grow healthy and strong. Our bodies also need oils. You should get your oils from foods such as fish, nuts, and liquid oils.

 Read the words in the box. Color the food pyramid to match.

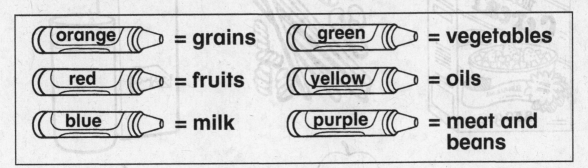

orange = grains   green = vegetables

red = fruits   yellow = oils

blue = milk   purple = meat and beans

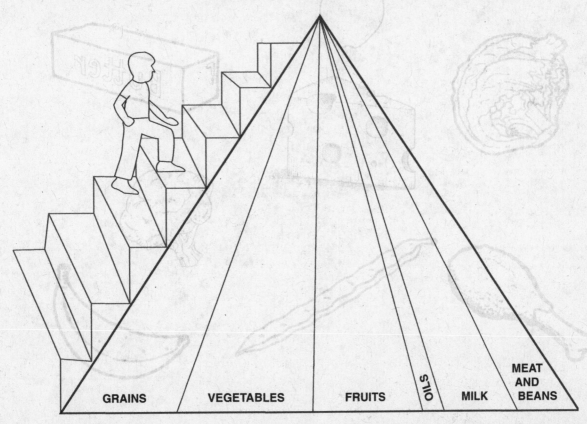

GRAINS   VEGETABLES   FRUITS   OILS   MILK   MEAT AND BEANS

Go on to the next page.

Health, Nutrition, and P.E. 1–2, SV 1419023578

The Food Pyramid, p. 2

 Color the foods below. Use the colors in the box on page 67 to show the section of the pyramid each food belongs in.

Health, Nutrition, and P.E. 1–2, SV 1419023578

Name _____ Date _____

The Food Pyramid Web Site

There is a web site that tells about the food pyramid. You can visit the site at this Internet address: www.MyPyramid.gov. It will tell you how much of each food to eat so you can be healthy. The man on the steps helps you remember to exercise every day.

 Follow the directions to find the food pyramid that is just right for you.

Step 1: Type in this address in the bar: www.MyPyramid.gov.

Step 2: Look on the right side of the screen. Find the box that says My Pyramid Plan.

Step 3: Find the word Age. Type your age in the box under the word.

Step 4: Find the word Sex. Click on the arrows. If you are a boy, choose Male. If you are a girl, choose Female.

Step 5: Find the words Physical Activity. Click on the arrows. How much exercise do you get every day? Choose the words.

Step 6: Click on the word SUBMIT. Watch the screen change.

 Look at the numbers that tell how much of each food you should eat every day. Write the numbers in the chart below.

Foods	How Much to Eat
Grains	_____ ounces
Vegetables	_____ cups
Fruits	_____ cups
Oils	_____ teaspoons
Milk	_____ cups
Meat and Beans	_____ ounces

(Hints: A number that ends in .5 stands for $\frac{1}{2}$ cup. The chart does not tell how many teaspoons of oil to eat. You will need to look below the chart.)

Go on to the next page.

Health, Nutrition, and P.E. 1–2, SV 1419023578

The Food Pyramid Web Site, p. 2

Look at the completed chart on page 69. Find the column with the heading <u>How Much to Eat</u>. It tells how much of each food you should eat every day.

 Color the measuring tools to show how much of each food you should eat each day. For the scales, color a scale to show I ounce. For the cups, color the cup to show I full cup or a $\frac{1}{2}$ cup.

Foods	How Much to Eat
Grains (in ounces)	
Vegetables (in cups)	
Fruits (in cups)	
Oils (in teaspoons)	
Milk (in cups)	
Meat and Beans (in ounces)	

Health, Nutrition, and P.E. 1–2, SV 1419023578

My Food Pyramid Game

 Color each part of the cube to show the colors on the food pyramid.

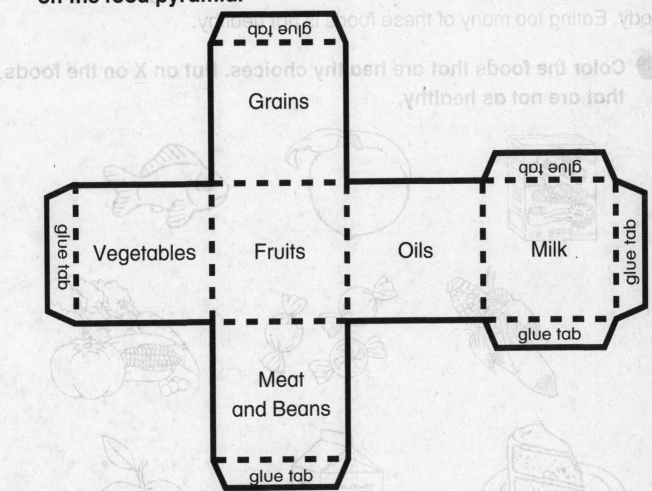

glue tab

Grains

glue tab

glue tab

Vegetables | Fruits | Oils | Milk

glue tab

Meat and Beans

glue tab

 Play this game with a friend.

Get a copy of page 70 that you colored. Look at how much of each food you should eat each day. Next get a copy of page 70 that has not been colored. Take turns rolling the cube. Color one scale each time the grains or meat and beans colors show. Color $\frac{1}{2}$ cup each time the vegetables, fruits, or milk colors show. Color one teaspoon each time the oil color shows. Continue rolling the cube and coloring the measurement tools until you reach the amounts shown for you on page 70. If you roll a color you do not need, skip that turn.

Health, Nutrition, and P.E. 1–2, SV 1419023578

Name _____ Date _____

Making Healthy Food Choices

Many foods are good for you to eat. They give you things your body needs for good health. Some food choices are NOT as good for your body. Eating too many of these foods is not healthy.

 Color the foods that are healthy choices. Put an X on the foods that are not as healthy.

Health, Nutrition, and P.E. 1–2, SV 1419023578

Name _____ Date _____

Fats in Foods

Fats are found in many foods. Limit the solid fats you eat, such as butter, stick margarine, and shortening. Also limit the foods you eat that contain solid fats. Read the Nutrition Facts label on foods to find out how much fat they contain.

 Materials
- brown paper bag
- scissors
- foods to test

 Do this

A. Cut the paper bag into 3-inch squares. Write the name of each food you wish to test on a different square.

B. Rub a piece of food on a square until it leaves a wet spot. If the food is liquid, put a drop of it on the square.

C. Set the squares aside to dry.

D. When the squares dry, hold them up to the light. If there is a greasy spot, the food contains fat. Fill in the chart below.

FOOD	FAT	NO FAT
milk		

 Answer the question.

How can you find out how much fat is in a glass of milk? _____

_____

Health, Nutrition, and P.E. 1–2, SV 1419023578

Name _____ Date _____

Name _____ Date _____

Snack Attack!

Sometimes, you might be hungry between meals. It is best to choose snacks that are good for your body.

 Under each picture, write the first letter of the name of the picture.

1.

2.

3.

 Read the letters in each line to find a good decision you can make about food.

Health, Nutrition, and P.E. 1–2, SV 1419023578

Name _____ Date _____

Food Diary

 List the foods you eat in one day. Write them in the column in which they belong.

	Breakfast	Lunch	Dinner	Snacks
Meat and Beans				
Milk				
Fruits				
Vegetables				
Grains				

Name _____ Date _____

Eating Out

∞∞

It is fun to go out to eat. You can make good food choices that are healthy.

 Look at the restaurant menu. Choose something from each section. Circle your choices. Choose a healthful lunch.

Soups	**Desserts**
Chicken and rice	Frozen yogurt
Tomato	Hot fudge sundae
Vegetable chili	Strawberries
	Frozen juice bar
Drinks	Oatmeal raisin cookies
Caffeine-free cola	
Lemonade	**Extras**
Milk	Fries
Orange juice	Chips and dip
Apple juice	Applesauce
	Coleslaw
Sandwiches	Carrots and celery
Tuna salad	Green salad
Grilled cheese	
Fried fish	
Turkey	
Hot dog	
Veggie burger	

∞∞

Health, Nutrition, and P.E. 1–2, SV 1419023578

Tia's Shopping Trip

ORANGES 99¢
APPLES 89¢
59¢

Tia likes to help her mom shop for food. Tia knows that choosing healthy foods will give her the energy she needs to be active.

1

Fold

Activity

Make a shopping list. List three healthy foods or drinks that you like. Make one of your choices something that helps you get the water you need.

Shopping List

4

Unit 2: Nutrition
Health, Nutrition, and P.E. 1–2, SV 1419023578

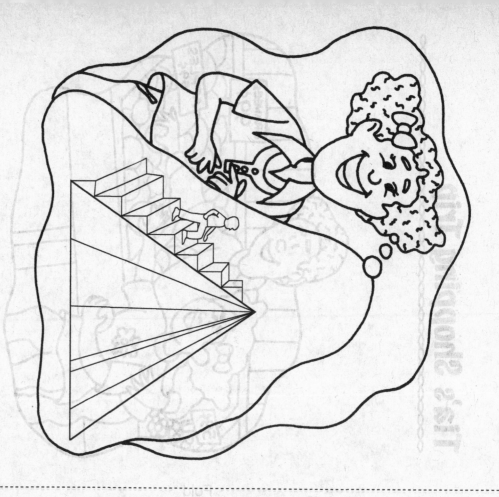

Before they go shopping, Tia and her mother plan meals for the week. They use the Food Pyramid. They choose healthy foods. Then Tia helps her mother make a shopping list.

2

Tia and her mom know it is important to drink a lot of water. They buy juice and milk because they can get some of the water they need from these drinks.

Tia and her mom shop carefully. They read food labels. Tia knows to watch out for too much fat, salt, or sugar.

3

Unit 2: Nutrition
Health, Nutrition, and P.E. 1–2, SV 1419023578

Teacher Resource

Exercising has many healthful benefits. First, muscles grow when they are used. Unexercised muscles contract when they are not used. Muscles that become unaccustomed to exercise can be injured by sudden or strenuous activity. This is why muscles, including the heart, should be exercised regularly and in moderation. Occasional strenuous activity is not advantageous to the muscles and does not give long-term results.

Moreover, exercise also controls weight and increases endurance and strength. Regular exercise can also relax the body, reduce stress, and help people get a good night's sleep. Finally, exercise can reduce the rate of premature mortality, including heart disease, hypertension, and colon cancer.

Since schools are often financially restricted, the physical education curriculum is considered less important. The classroom teacher must provide rich and varied experiences for students so they can exercise as well as learn how to establish and maintain a healthy lifestyle. Teachers are responsible for developing a wide variety of activities that promote basic movement skills; games for individuals, partners, and teams; physical fitness; and dance. Teachers also need to ensure that each student achieves his or her optimum mental, emotional, social, and physical development. This is a tall order when the curriculum is already packed with the need to teach core subjects.

The activities and ideas below offer some fun, creative ways to enrich your physical education program, while developing important health goals.

Individual

Letter Jump   Write the alphabet or numbers on index cards and tape them securely to the floor. Call out one locomotive skill (hop, jump, walk, run) and have children find and move to that card. (Students can move in order or to a skill, such as to the card that has the beginning sound or even or odd number pattern.)

Simon Says Body   Make sure students can accurately identify left and right. Then call out left and right body parts that students must touch on themselves. For example, students might touch left elbow to right ankle, or right ear to right foot. Challenge students to be creative in their movements, and remind them they can sit or stand to accomplish the task.

Pattern Moving   Call out actions quickly, such as "Clap your hands" or "Jump on the right foot." Students complete each movement. Gradually increase the number of instructions that students follow so that students are making four or five movements in a row.

The Bouncing Beat   Invite students to choose a ball. Then play different music selections that have a strong beat. Point out the rhythm in each.

Health, Nutrition, and P.E. 1–2, SV 1419023578

Challenge students to dribble the ball to the beat. During transition to other music, you may wish to invite students to try different kinds of creative dribbling, such as bounce and spin once, or behind the back.

Pairs or Small Groups

Mirror Me   Have partners face each other. One student is the "image" and the other is the "reflection." The image moves in different ways for the reflection to mirror. Remind students to move slowly to stay in unison.

On a Roll   Cover a box with craft paper and label each side with a body part. Working in small groups sitting in circles, students take turns rolling the box and designating which parts to touch to the floor.

Squirrel Races   Crumple one brown sack for each student. Then spread the sacks on the floor in the middle of the play area. Place a box at each end of the room. Remind students that squirrels often store acorns so they have food during the cold winter months. Then divide the class into two teams and place a team on each side of the play area. Explain that the sacks are acorns, the box is the storage area, and the students will be the squirrels. Tell students they must take turns running to an acorn and picking it up with their chin. Then they carry the acorn back to the box and drop it in the storage area. No hands are permitted. The first team that has each squirrel successfully retrieve an acorn wins.

Station to Station   Set up a variety of fun activity stations. You might include balls, ropes, hoops, and even tricycles! Then divide the class into groups of four or five. Make one less group than the number of stations. Come up with creative activities students can do while in the stations. Keep the time short so students have to organize and begin the activity quickly.

The Hungry Caterpillar   Gather four of a variety of items, such as small balls, books, or paper clips. Try to get at least eight different items. Spread the items out in a large, cleared area on the floor. Then divide the class into four caterpillar teams. Have them stand in line, one behind the other, and use the left or right hand to hold the shoulder of the person in front. The first person is the "head" of the caterpillar, and the last person is the "tail." Give the tail a plastic grocery sack. On a designated signal, have each caterpillar team move around the floor collecting one of each item in a set amount of time. The head must pick up each item and pass it down the line to the tail. Students cannot disconnect, or all the items in the bag must be removed and the team starts again. The first team to gather all the items yells "butterfly."

Large Group

Speed Ball   Have all students stand by their desks. Assign a category, such as an animal sound, machine noise, or television show. Students toss a ball to classmates and make the sound or name the item without repeats as they catch the ball. If students repeat sounds or cannot say something, they sit down and are out of the game.

Health, Nutrition, and P.E. 1–2, SV 1419023578

Parachute Number Change Assign each student a number. Then have all students hold the edges of a parachute at waist level. Call out two or three numbers. Students having those numbers go under the parachute and exchange places.

On the Hot Seat Have students sit in a circle on the floor or in chairs. One student gets the "hot seat" in the middle. Call out any characteristic that could relate to students, for example, students wearing green, students whose first name begins with s, students who have birthdays in May, etc. If the descriptor applies to the student, he or she gets up and runs to a seat vacated by another student. The person in the hot seat also tries to find another seat. The student left standing is now on the hot seat.

Hoop It Up Gather 10 hoops. Have 10 students stand about 36 inches apart and hold the hoops vertically to the ground at any height so that the base of the hoop is no more than knee height. Next, invite the other students to move through the hoops without touching them. When the last person in line moves through the hoops, the tenth student puts the hoop down and moves through the 9 hoops. The ninth person then puts the hoop down and moves through 8 hoops, and so on, until all 10 hoops are on the ground. The next 10 students in line pick up the hoops and the course begins again. Challenge students to complete each round quickly.

You're a Star Tag Cut out stars from yellow paper and tape them securely on the floor. Invite several volunteers to be a "star" and stand on a star cutout. Have the remaining students move to one end of the play area. Tell them they are "rockets." Lead stars in a countdown: "3, 2, 1, blastoff!" The rockets move through the stars to the other side of the play area. Stars must keep one foot on the star while trying to tag the rockets. Each tagged rocket "loses power" and stops. They become stars and select a star to stand on. Play continues until all the rockets have been tagged.

Health, Nutrition, and P.E. 1–2, SV 1419023578

Bulletin Board: All Aboard the Exercise Express!

Materials

engine pattern (page 83)   craft paper   glue

train car pattern (page 83)   construction paper   scissors

ticket patterns (page 83)   envelopes   stapler

Teacher Directions

1. Prepare a bulletin board with the desired color of craft paper. Add the title "All Aboard the Exercise Express!"
2. Cut the flap off an envelope. Staple the envelop, with the "v" side showing, to one corner of the board.
3. Duplicate the engine on red construction paper. Cut it out and staple it to the board.
4. Duplicate several cars. Cut them out to use as patterns.
5. Duplicate many tickets. Cut them out and place them in the envelope.
6. Set a course for students to run or walk. You might choose the perimeter of the playground or a field. Students will get a ticket each time they travel the distance.
7. Decide how many tickets must be earned before students can make a car to be added to the train on the board. Write each student's name on an envelope. Store the envelopes in a place where students can store their tickets.
8. Challenge students to build a very long train. Suggest that they run or walk the course daily. Give them a ticket each time they complete one lap. When they reach the predetermined number of tickets, allow them to make a train car.
9. Staple the train cars to the board.

Student Directions

1. Choose a color of construction paper. Trace a train car on it. Cut out the car.
2. Draw two circles on black paper for train wheels. Cut them out. Glue them on the car.
3. Glue your tickets on the car.

Health, Nutrition, and P.E. 1–2, SV 1419023578

Bulletin Board Patterns

Engine

Train Car

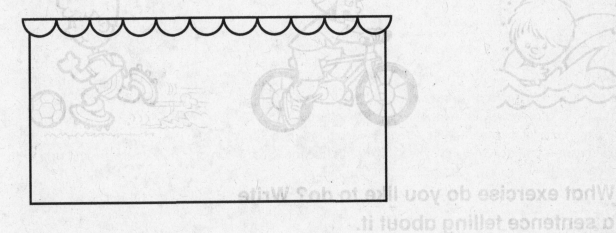

Tickets

Health, Nutrition, and P.E. 1–2, SV 1419023578

Name _____ Date _____

Exercise and You

Exercise helps you build a strong body. It can help make your muscles stronger. Some exercises make you breathe deeply. They make your heart beat fast. Exercise helps your heart do its job better.

 Color the pictures that show someone who is exercising.

 What exercise do you like to do? Write a sentence telling about it.

_____

_____

Health, Nutrition, and P.E. 1–2, SV 1419023578

Name _____ Date _____

Warming Up and Cooling Down

It is important to warm up your body before you exercise. The muscles will work better. Then you will not hurt your muscles. You need to cool down after exercising, too. It will help your muscles rest. Stretching is the best way to warm up and cool down. Follow these tips when you stretch.

- Never bounce. Stretch gently.
- Breathe normally to get the air you need.
- Never stretch until it hurts. You should only feel a slight pull.

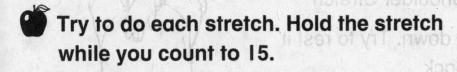 **Try to do each stretch. Hold the stretch while you count to 15.**

I. Shoulder and Chest Stretch

Pull your hands slowly toward the floor. Keep your elbows straight but don't lock them.

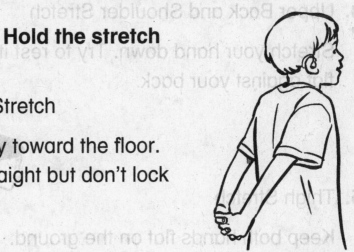

2. Sit and Reach Stretch

Bend forward at the waist. Keep your eyes on your toes.

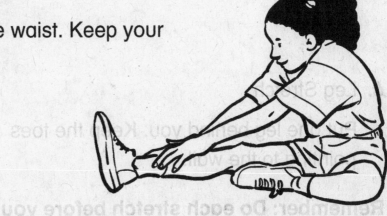

Go on to the next page.

Unit 3: P.E.
Health, Nutrition, and P.E. 1–2, SV 1419023578

Warming Up and Cooling Down, p. 2

3. Calf Stretch

Keep both feet on the floor. Move
your feet apart if you need to get a
better stretch.

4. Upper Back and Shoulder Stretch

Stretch your hand down. Try to rest it
flat against your back.

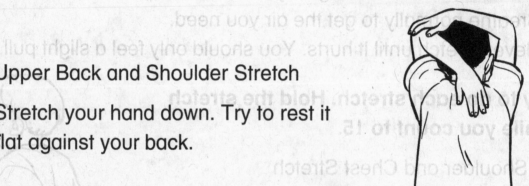

5. Thigh Stretch

Keep both hands flat on the ground.
Lean as far forward as you can.

6. Leg Stretch

Put one leg behind you. Keep the toes
pointing to the wall.

**Remember: Do each stretch before you
exercise. Do the same stretches again
after you exercise.**

Name _____ Date _____

Build Your Heart and Lungs

Exercise helps your heart and lungs grow strong. You should exercise for at least 60 minutes every day, or most days. You want to make your heart beat faster. You want to get lots of air in your lungs.

🍎 **Look at the pictures. They show some exercises that are good for your body. Write the name of the exercise under each picture.**

jump	dance	swim	run	skate	ride

1.

_____

2.

_____

3.

_____

4.

_____

5.

_____

6.

_____

Favorite Ways to Exercise

You can get exercise in many different ways. Some people go to the gym. They like to exercise alone. Some people like to play soccer. They like to exercise with others. All exercise helps to make the body healthy.

🍎 **What is your favorite kind of exercise?**
Complete the sentence.

My favorite kind of exercise is _____.

🍎 **What kind of exercises do your friends like?**
Take a poll. Write the answers in the chart.

Name	Favorite Kind of Exercise

Unit 3: P.E.
Health, Nutrition, and P.E. 1–2, SV 1419023578

Name _____ Date _____

Manage Stress with Exercise

Sometimes you might feel worried, or stressed. Too much bad stress can hurt your body. There are some things you can do to get rid of the stress. Some people exercise. It helps the worried or uncomfortable feelings to go away.

 Draw lines to show the correct order of the steps you can take to get rid of stress.

Numbers	Steps
Step 1	**A.** Take one step at a time.
Step 2	**B.** Think about ways to get rid of the stress.
Step 3	**C.** Do the things that will get rid of the stress.
Step 4	**D.** Know how stress feels.

 Draw your favorite way to get rid of stress.

Health, Nutrition, and P.E. 1–2, SV 1419023578

Fitness Mountain

 **How quickly can you get to the top of Fitness Mountain?
Write the kind of exercise you do each time. Remember,
you must exercise at least 60 minutes to count the exercise.**

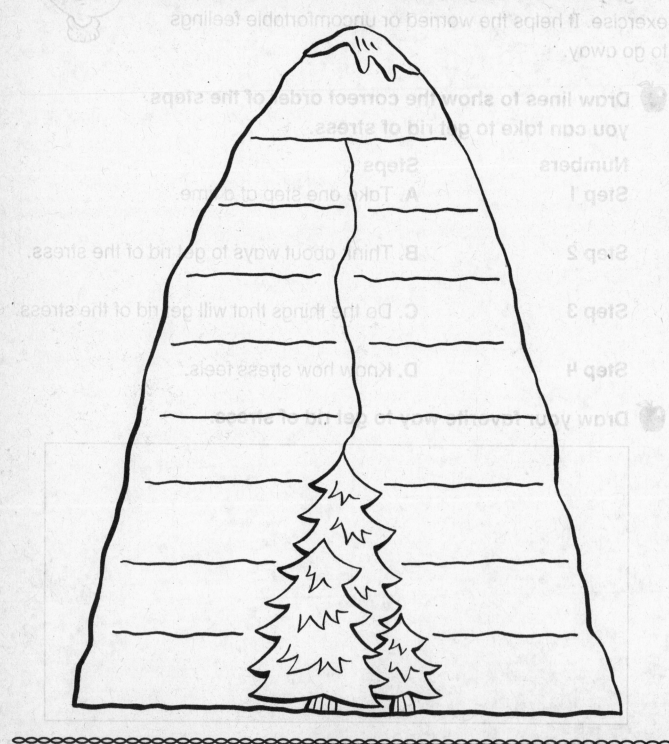

Health, Nutrition, and P.E. 1–2, SV 1419023578

Fancy Footwork Exercise

🍎 **Look at the footprints. One is the left foot. One is the right foot. Cut out the footprints. Trace several of each on paper. Cut them out. Put them on the floor to make a jumping pattern to use for exercise. Ask a partner to follow the pattern.**

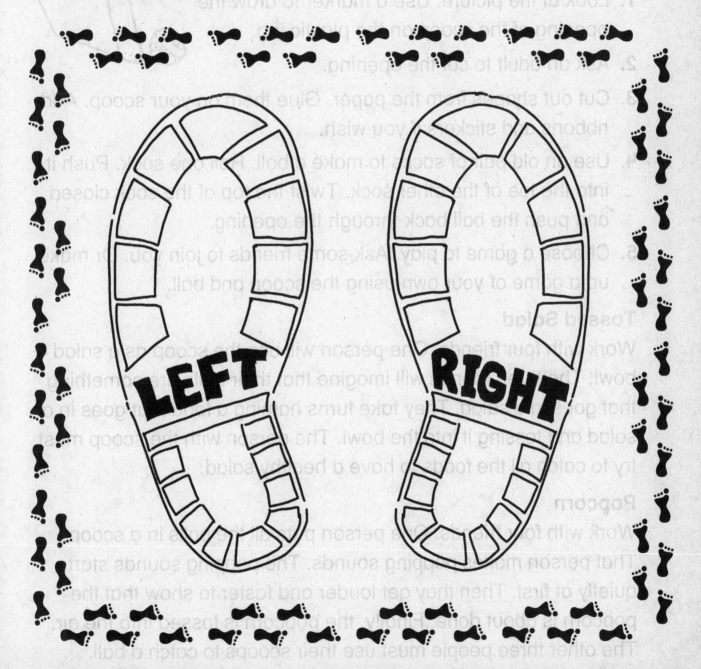

Health, Nutrition, and P.E. 1–2, SV 1419023578

Super Scooper

 Materials
- plastic gallon jug • construction paper • stickers • ribbons
- an old pair of socks • scissors • permanent marker • glue

 Do This

1. Look at the picture. Use a marker to draw the opening of the scoop on the plastic jug.

2. Ask an adult to cut the opening.

3. Cut out shapes from the paper. Glue them on your scoop. Add ribbons and stickers if you wish.

4. Use an old pair of socks to make a ball. Roll one sock. Push it into the toe of the other sock. Twist the top of the sock closed and push the ball back through the opening.

5. Choose a game to play. Ask some friends to join you. Or make up a game of your own using the scoop and ball.

Tossed Salad

Work with four friends. One person will use the scoop as a salad bowl. The three friends will imagine that their balls are something that goes in a salad. They take turns naming a food that goes in a salad and tossing it into the bowl. The person with the scoop must try to catch all the foods to have a healthy salad.

Popcorn

Work with four friends. One person puts all the balls in a scoop. That person makes popping sounds. The popping sounds start quietly at first. Then they get louder and faster to show that the popcorn is about done. Finally, the popcorn is tossed into the air. The other three people must use their scoops to catch a ball.

Health, Nutrition, and P.E. 1–2, SV 1419023578

Fitness Fun

Rueben gets lots of exercise. He loves to move around. Sometimes he runs and plays with friends. Rueben likes karate best of all.

1

Fold

Activity

What do you like to do for exercise? Draw a picture of yourself doing the exercise.

4

Health, Nutrition, and P.E. 1–2, SV 1419023578

Ken likes to skate best of all. He also likes to exercise with his family. They go for a long walk together.

Ella looks forward to playtime at school each day. It is a good time for her to exercise. She can run and swing. She can play on the monkey bars. Today Ella decides to jump rope.

2

Lin and Jill are friends. They joined a soccer team to get exercise. They go to practice two times each week. They play a game each Saturday.

3

94

Unit 3: P.E.
Health, Nutrition, and P.E. 1–2, SV 1419023578

Answer Key

Page 5
1. B
2. D
3. C
4. B
5. D
6. A
7. C
8. A

Page 6
9. C
10. A
11. C
12. D

Page 11
Accept reasonable drawings.

Page 12
Answers will vary.

Page 13
A. 6
B. 3
C. 1
D. 5
E. 2
F. 4

Page 14
Answers will vary.

Page 15
Answers will vary.

Page 16
Bodies Growing: A, C, H
Learning Things: B, D, F
Being Responsible: E, G, I

Page 17
Answers will vary.

Page 18
Answers will vary.

Page 19
1. C
2. A
3. D
4. B

Page 20
Answers will vary.

Page 21
1. A
2. B
3. A

Page 22
Step 1 Stop.
Step 2 Agree to disagree.
Step 3 Talk about a solution.
Step 4 Find a way for both sides to win.

Page 23
1. Students draw a line to the mouth.
2. Students draw a line to the hand.
3. Students draw a line to the eyes.
4. Students draw a line to the nose.
5. Students draw a line to the ear.

Page 24
1. A. Students draw a line to the pupil.
   B. Students draw a line to the white part surrounding the pupil. Students color the irises to match their eye color. Students color the pupils black.
2. Students draw pupils that are large.
3. Students draw pupils that are small.
4. Possible answer: They help us see.

Page 25
1. Students draw a line to the girl's back.
2. Students draw a line to the girl's head.
3. Students draw a line to the girl's arm.
4. Students draw a line to the girl's foot.
5. Students draw a line to the girl's chest.
Students draw kneepads.

Page 26
Possible answer: The tubes are the bones. The rubber band and the balloon are the muscles. The muscles and bones work together to make the elbow move.

Page 27
1. muscles
2. nerves
3. nerves
4. muscles
5. nerves

Page 28
1. B
2. C
3. D
4. A

Page 29
Saliva started breaking down the cracker.

Page 30
Check that students color the heart and blood vessels red.

Page 31
The heartbeat gets faster with movement.

Page 32
Check that students color the parts of the tooth correctly.
Question: enamel

Page 33
Order: 1, 3, 2
Answers will vary.

Page 34
Students circle the milk, toothpaste, toothbrush, girl brushing teeth, dentist, and fruit.

Page 35
Answers will vary.

Page 36
Answers will vary.

Page 37
1. wash
2. teeth
3. food
4. bed

Page 38
1. The girl uses a tissue to sneeze or cough so that germs are not spread.
2. The girl is keeping her hair clean so germs will be removed.
3. The girl is washing her face to remove germs.
4. Possible answers: wash hands, brush teeth, brush hair, wear clean clothes.

Page 39
1. T
2. T
3. T
4. F
5. F
6. Possible answers: You cannot see germs. Fingernails need to be cleaned and trimmed.

Answer Key
Health, Nutrition, and P.E. 1–2, SV 1419023578

Answer Key *continued*

Answer Key

Page 40
Children circle the boy saying no to food, the girl with the thermometer, and the boy sneezing.

Page 41
1. B
2. E
3. A
4. D
5. C

Page 42
Across
1. allergy
3. head lice
4. vaccines
Down
1. asthma
2. disease
5. ill

Page 43
1. B
2. A
3. D
4. C
5. E

Page 44
Answers will vary.
Accept reasonable drawings.

Page 45
1. B
2. A

Page 46
1. caffeine
2. instructions
3. medicines, medicines
4. drugs

Page 47
Check that students color the parts of the mouth correctly.

Page 48
Answers will vary.

Page 49
Answers will vary.

Page 50
Answers will vary.

Page 52
Students circle the following: newspapers near the fire, open fireplace, television near the fire, cord running in front of fire, pillow near the electric heater, overused plug, toys on stairs.

Page 53
Answers will vary, but make sure students give specific information of full name, full address, and information about what they do know.

Page 54
Students write *stop, drop,* and *roll* under the corresponding picture and glue them in the correct order.

Page 55
Outlets are often at the eye level of small children. Some children may stick things into the outlets and hurt themselves.

Page 56
1. The boy should not be sticking anything into an outlet. The electricity can move through the screwdriver and through his body.
2. The girl should not be using an appliance with wet hands. Electricity can move through water and hurt her.

Page 57
Students circle the girl using a hand signal and the boy riding at night with lights and a helmet. Students put an *X* on the child biking across the street with a red light in her direction and the boy riding on the street in between cars.

Page 58
1. C
2. D
3. A
4. B

Page 59
1. B
2. D
3. E
4. A
5. C

Page 60
1. X-ray; pictures of the inside of the body
2. surgery; having an operation

Page 67
Students should follow the code to correctly color the food pyramid.

Page 68
Students color the foods these colors:
Orange: noodles, cereal

Green: lettuce, broccoli
Red: banana, apple
Yellow: butter
Blue: milk, cheese
Purple: chicken, beans

Page 69
Answers will vary.

Page 70
Students' answers should match the numbers in their chart on page 69.

Page 71
Students color the cube to match the colors of the food pyramid.

Page 72
Students color the cereal, peach, fish, corn, vegetables, milk, apple, and eggs. Students put an *X* on the candy, soda, cake, and ice cream.

Page 73
Read the Nutrition Facts label on the milk container.

Page 74
1. choose
2. healthy
3. snacks

Page 75
Answers will vary.

Page 76
Answers will vary.

Page 84
Students color the ball player, swimmer, biker, and soccer player.

Page 87
1. skate
2. swim
3. ride
4. dance
5. run
6. jump

Page 88
Answers will vary.

Page 89
Step 1: D
Step 2: B
Step 3: A
Step 4: C

Page 90
Answers will vary.

Health, Nutrition, and P.E. 1–2, SV 1419023578